A GOSPEL OF BONES

A GOSPEL
OF BONES

POEMS

SUZI Q. SMITH

Alternating Current Press
Boulder, Colorado

A Gospel of Bones
Suzi Q. Smith
©2021 Alternating Current Press

All material in *A Gospel of Bones* is the property of its respective creator and may not be used or reprinted in any manner without express permission from the author or publisher, except for the quotation of short passages used inside of an article, criticism, or review. Printed in the United States of America. All rights reserved. All material in *A Gospel of Bones* is printed with permission.

Alternating Current
Boulder, Colorado
press.alternatingcurrentarts.com

ISBN: 978-1-946580-27-6
First Edition: February 2021

This book is dedicated to my ancestors and my descendants.
To my daughter, my mother, my grandmother, my siblings.
To my aunties, my uncles, my cousins.
To my friends. To my loves. To Park Hill and the Eastside.
To the church choir. To the praise team.
To my grandmother's piano.
To Colorado Boulevard.
To How I Got Over and I've Come Too Far to Turn Around.
To Where Could I Go.
To This Joy That I Found.
To the verses who have opened into homes.
To the gospel of and in my bones.

TABLE OF CONTENTS

We Pay Cash for Houses 13
This Crown Crooked Anyway 14
You Scared? 28
Aquemini: A Gospel 29
We Don't Really Say That Word 32
Bones 34
Imitation of Hope 36
FDT 38
Homegirl 39
Ars Poetica 42
Some People Like Me Better as an Idea 43
You Can('t) Take Us Anywhere 45
A Primary Education in Sex 48
Me Too 49
Clumsy-Tongued Lovers 51
How to Get a Man Out of Your House 53
Lucky 54
The House of Joy 55
The God Conjurers Sing 57
The Blue Note Bends 'til Breaking 59
Éostre 60
Mustangs 61
Sweetback 64
Load 68
On the Day You Visit a Slaughterhouse 70
Divorce Cake: A Recipe 73
Cecil 76
I Fall in Love at Museums 78
My Stepfather Is Not the Kind of Man Who Weeps 79
I Do Not Know How to Love You in English 80
For Cedric 83
My Father's Hands 86
Black Rage in Four-Part Harmony 89

A GOSPEL
OF BONES

WE PAY CASH FOR HOUSES

Front yards with grass,
old trees and shiny crab apples
liquor stores here got bulletproof glass
the churches, tattered lighthouses
hold all our secrets
we lost Martin Luther King Boulevard
we hum our shame in moans
old Spirituals shaped the bricks
hand-me-down houses
delicious trees that gossip over fences
Popeyes chicken, Church's chicken
Laundromat-check-cashing-payday-loans
we, who know each other's names
and borrowed cups of sugar
twenty dollars until payday
just until we get on our feet,
And did we not? Get on our feet?
We made this, all of this
We made it.

Fresh cut,
clean as first-day-of-school sneakers
even the mirrors finesse
the new banks on the block
bundles of slow plunder
but the sidewalks ain't cracked no more
the alleyways, smooth as untested promise
of former corner-store seedlings
blooming into downward-facing dog
and parks that unwelcome children,
bike lanes and boutique wine bars
or family-friendly microbreweries
hear all the scents and sounds conspiring,
flooding to the teeth in whispered howls,
drowning in hissed welcomes
adrift the taunting memory of ground.
Air, made fat and wet with our breath,
for you.
For you.

THIS CROWN CROOKED ANYWAY

I. The Rapture Came in the Early 90s

At church, they used to take the kids into the basement
to show us poor-made horror movies on The Rapture
remind us we don't want to be the ones they leave and
Jesus only wants the well-behaved so when the kids
around you start to disappear you better pray and
get right with The Lord and baby would you believe it?
Other kids began to slip off into Jesus' arms?

The Bible says, *"Train up a child in the way he should
go: and when he is old, he will not depart from it."*

You heard about that boy whose clothes were always dirty?
Flashed a gun all over seventh grade and disappeared.
I'm saying. You act like you don't see these empty seats.
I pray until my knees bruise, my knuckles tight glowing.
I'm singing "Pass Me Not" on my way back home from school.

II. Find a Sweet Relief

I'm still singing "Pass Me Not" on my way back home from school.
The walk is long, an exercise in faith and violence.
I tuck my chin, quick my pace, try not to be a target.
Who got the time to be somebody's victim anyway?

I've never been in a fight I wasn't dragged away from.
This is not to say that I won them, just that violence
is a language I have learned, inherited, and practiced.
A mother tongue always lies dormant in my mouth and blood.

"Stop all that before I give you something to cry about!"

One time, me and Genevieve fought Quinton on the same day.
I got up bloody again and then again, wild swinging
knowing the only one coming to save me is Jesus.
What if I am my only hero? What if you are yours?

You ever snatch your breath out the mouth of a barking dog?

III. They Called It the Summer of Violence

You ever snatch your breath out the mouth of a barking dog?

We grew up in the 80s, back when our blocks were still ours.
White flight had left the guts of cities to our grandparents.
There was a war on drugs. Nancy Reagan was on TV.

We lived with our grandmother and we wore hand-me-down clothes.
Used to brag about my wealthy father like I knew him,
pretend like I ain't have to share a bed with my cousin.

We were royal ancient children. We were "at-risk" youth.
We were young lords of the flies, wrestling our fate and future
inheritance from statistics. We learned to steel ourselves.

Do you remember the summer of 1993?
When the boys that we all used to know became murderers?
When all the girls began to know we would become widows?

"Blessed be the Lord my strength which teacheth my hands to war. ..."

IV. The Blister in Our Mother Tongue

"Blessed be the Lord my strength which teacheth my hands to war. ..."

Even children know how to light fires around here,
to gather tinder, flint, kindling. Is that power?
Will it make us safer? Will it keep our skin close?

You ever tried to sing or wail a wall into the ground?
Understand the pitch and force required to smash a window?
Considered what you know about kerosene and rags?

Haven't you ever damn near swallowed someone's knuckles?
Ain't had to pinch the bridge of your nose back into shape?
Smiled bloody, said "fine" before the scabs are even dry?

Haven't you ever had to ball your fists and swing?
Isn't everything we dream of an act of Self
Defense? Haven't you had your body colonized?

"Don't you start no fights, but best believe you can finish them."

V. Pretty Is as Pretty Does

"Don't you start no fights, but best believe you can finish them."

Didn't my mother's quilting teach me something about needles?
What do I know of womanhood but ripping seams and stitches?

Haven't I learned and taught how to divorce myself from myself?
Don't I know better than to drink with the hungry eyes of men?
Haven't I always haunted my tentative, gentle body?

Spreading, making some kind of home in this quarantined trigger
sutured and scarred from the survived sacrifice? See what I made?
With the ashes and the hammers I keep under my pillow?

I smear these ghosts all over my plump lips, tell me it's pretty.
What's the difference between a stomach and a heart, anyway?
I still don't know enough about hands to wear them correctly.

Sometimes I treat my buttery flesh like I'm just passing through.
After all, doesn't every place I go ask me where I'm from?

VI. My Address Is an Asterisk

I mean, doesn't every place I go ask me where I'm from
(as in when will I be going back wherever that is)?

And called me "exotic" like the word is a compliment
(not a one-way ticket back to someplace they haven't been)?

Aren't I always the guest invited tentatively?
Isn't my name placed in italics and parentheses?

Surely I have known a home and will mourn its erasure
which is, of course, hearing my Nana play the piano

and Aunt Dee out front honking the horn of her Cadillac.
It's true, all the places that knew me are disappearing

as fast as the people, but I ask: for whom shall I weep?
You, for losing something that you never knew was not yours?

Or for me, who never bothered to pretend it was mine?
"Do not forget where you come from. Remember who you are."

VII. Sometimes They Put Your Family in Cages

"Forget where you come from. Remember who you are."
My little cousin calls on a Wednesday evening
and I apologize for missing his court date
but Nana was in the hospital and he says
thank you for the money on my books and I say
your grandma's doing better since the heart attack
he asks if I will tell everyone he loves them
he asks if Nana's still mad about his tattoos
The DA offered him forty years if he pleads
he didn't even do it but he'll take twenty
if he can see his son again before he's grown
he asks "when I was little, did you ever think
I would end up here?" Our anchored blood pours heavy
when love is our only home and a mudslide too.

VIII. Middle Age Might as Well Be Paradise

When love is our only home and a mudslide too,
we dance and drown and bury ourselves in fistfuls.
Melvin got shot while driving his El Camino
on the same afternoon as my bridal shower.
He survived, was still a groomsman in our wedding.
Tariq didn't get his tux in time, but he still
came to the reception looking clean as ever.
A few years later he was killed at his front door.
Russ is skinny, but the cancer's in remission.
Maybe it was prayer, or maybe the chicken broth,
his belly almost looks like a place I once knew.
Dear God, I love seeing men I have loved get old
and grouchy, complain about new trends in hip hop.
Yes, I love the sweet silver whiskers in your beards.

IX. Future Single Mother

Yes, I love the sweet silver whiskers in your beards
and the topographical map of my own body.

This storyteller belly remembers and tells
how we became and unbecame a family,
pinpoints the moment I learned she was here, I was
nineteen and afraid of the ways that I would fail her,

so I said yes when he asked me to be his wife,
an uncharted territory we pioneered
now marked in our dimmer skin, rising and falling,
this crevice between my brows, divorcing my face.

When I packed our daughter's tiny clothes quietly
no one applauded the grace of my departure,
spoke north and south of our unkeyed journey, though once
we were so in love, we watered our hope with sweat.

X. I Hope the Building Is Haunted

We were so in love then, we watered our hope with sweat.
The summer of '99 we were freshly married,
my ankles swole, belly full of dreams and our daughter.
Remember Mr. Cousins owned the eastside back then?
When it was all still black but the vultures were perching?
We ran the 715, my husband pouring drinks
while I traded him kisses for my jambalaya.
Everybody's auntie was in there. Watching, winking.
The jukebox hadn't changed since the 70s, back when
people believed in a love like ours, before money
set the whole hood ablaze to disremember us well,
and the 715 opened with a polished face.
You can still see Zona's Tamales in its grimace
at a red light among the ruins of the eastside.

XI. I Still Go to the DMV on the Eastside

When stopped at a red light among the ruins of the eastside:

"You went to Manual?" and I said, "Nah." Dismissed this as a
half-attempted holla 'til I saw and knew his face, now grown.
I said, "Gove, huh?" and smiled. He said, "That's right, I knew I
      knew you."

We nodded affirmations, recognized the haunted pause,
and-do-you-remember-all-the-people-that-we-used-to-know?
People disappear so quiet, leave us talking to ourselves.
We say, "Nah, I just saw him" when we learn about a new death
or sentence. What kind of a war is this, refusing its own name?
Our names bleed into the headlines. What constitutes a war crime?
So far, I haven't murdered anyone. Praise the Lord two times.
"Ay Sis, you keepin it up," he said, when pulled up at the light,
"A lot of us back from Gove ain't really lookin good, you know?"

I howl and the tombstones in my teeth quiver, "I know you right."

XII. "You Know How They Do"
and Other African-American Proverbs

"I know you right." I howl and the tombstones in my teeth quiver
lamentations: *"You know once they get you, they like to keep you"*
and other oft-shared cautionary tales about our losses

did not keep our DeShawn from the front page of the *Denver Post*
once they decided his teenaged body threatened tourism

COULD THE PUBLIC PLEASE BE VIGILANT AND IF YOU SEE SOMETHING
SAY SOMETHING DO NOT APPROACH THE SUSPECT MAY BE DANGEROUS

and my phone ringing from people who of course want all the tea
but they have never known hot water hot blocks or hot corners

they got no skin in the game but quick to tell a good story.
I'm praying with my family they don't shoot him when they find him.

We're living on the losing side of war but no one calls it.
Watching cages and concrete swallow classmates, little cousins,

and even I only got – can only give – these here poems.

XIII. We All We Got

And even I only got can only give these poems.
Ain't sucked teeth side eye and doubt made the music I march to?
For haven't we perfected the power of poverty?
Didn't I shun ranks of women I was too smart to join?
Didn't they roll eyes, exasperated when I showed up?
Don't chitlins imply an embarrassment of our riches?
Ain't pride a cumbersome and hungry hog, always rooting?
Don't we know the might of beggary? The shame of it all?
Didn't we dance with statistics like we were being paid?
Haven't we been standing in these long lines, small as we can?
Didn't they always call me a horse-mule, bred to carry?
Wasn't I fool enough to hope for love? Celebration
for the joy brewed in my body, heavy and glistening,
when speaking to my lover on a rainy afternoon?

XIV. Set It Off

When speaking to my lover on a rainy afternoon,
he and I agree that we both mean everything we say,
and we believe enough of what we know between us, so
it would be too much weight for us to own or carry guns
while people (who have names and addresses) are, at best,
grinning widespread in discomfort, indifferent to our breath.
Baby, what if we believe in pre-emptive self-defense?

And if you've never seen a face flash quick against the shine
of letter opener and speculated severance,
you might be differently cornered than my lover and I
who've neutered our own edges just enough to hide the nerve
and I curve my fist my lips my grip around his trigger

and these wet thighs just might be all that's keeping me alive
and these wet thighs just might be all that's keeping you alive.

YOU SCARED?

if fear
is an accepted legal defense
for murder
how many times might I have killed?
how many times have I quaked and trembled?

how many times have I been
the only woman in the room?
the only black person in the room?
the only black woman in the room?
how many times has that fear
been justified?
(see: history. see yesterday.)

imagine
if I defended myself with fire next time.
every time.
how many fears could I kill in a day?
how many shadows would bleed out?

you scared?
me too.

AQUEMINI: A GOSPEL

Then David, also the youngest,
heard some giant was running his mouth
about his only God his father's God
his brothers all shaking at the war
but David loved his father's
God so fiercely he hollered how dare
and left that giant silently reflecting
on the miracle of rocks and
from this devotion of shit-talking
and fearless blood I am born
into love that marinates the shrimp
in butter and garlic leaves the rice to
stew slow in wet tomatoes traces the veins
on the chiles inspects the sunken stems and leaves
the seeds in because I know how you like it
to burn before you press a buttered roll between
your lips or me and go on to eat it all
and leave none for me and what kind of a god
does that? Not god, an endless swallow
of sky spitting rocks to fit the curl
of my leather sling – or hallowed hands,
onion-chopping-knee-rubbing-pot-scrubbing-weapons
pressed into each other in prayer:

>   the windows down we listened to Outkast's
>   new album *Aquemini* on repeat all the way
>   to Mississippi and back, memorizing and
>   rhyming the epilogue of our impending vows
> *When y'all gon' break up? When y'all gon' wake up?*

>   I loved him like David loved stones.
>   I loved him like Sisyphus loved stones.
> *The next four years you & somebody's daughter*
> *Raisin' y'all own young'n now that's a beautiful thang*
> *That's if you're on top of your game*
> *And man enough to handle real life situations (that is).*

I am not used to seeing him open, blood so easy to fetch.
> *Hold On, Be Strong*

do you want me to call your mother I will tell her not to come
do you want me to tell her the truth or lie
> *There's a fine line between love and hate you see*
> *Came way too late but baby I'm on it*

do you want me to call your insurance about the treatment
do you have insurance
> *… my fault, forget to mention*
> *You don't even have a checking account wasn't thinking about no pension*

do you want me to bring you food I used to make for you
do you want me to tell the nurses not to look at you with pity
> *grab her by her neck, throw her on the wall*
> *say bitch don't ever disrespect me never not at all*

do you want me to tell the doctors that you are not stupid
do you want me to apologize to them for your howling rage
> *If you scared, say you scared*

do you want me to give you my blood
do you want me to pull the plug
do you want me to put these rocks in my pocket or yours
do you want me to ask my grandmother to pray to David's God
> *Faith is what you make it that's the hardest shit since MC Ren*

the prayer stands for all things:
> *As long as there's that "tic tic" followed by that bump*

here, the war-willed wailing
there, the mallet into meat
when, I am a hunger talking to itself
then, I am a faithful mouth
> *I'm sorry y'all I often drift*

clean as hospital light and corners
crisp as clipboard and clipped voices
clinical and measured medicine
> *I said what you wanna be*
> *she said "Alive"*
> *I said what you wanna be*
> *he said "Alive"*
> *I said what you wanna be*
> *we said "Alive"*

I am not his wife anymore.
I am my mother's smallness, my grandmother's dutiful religion.
> *Shake that load off, shake that load off*

Of course I still pray for his family
we were young and unshaking and fierce
in love we hollered with pockets full of weapons
of course well-practiced aim and from this
devotion of shit-talking and fearless blood
I am born into grace that remembers to forget
the details of the war, my haunted hands
pressed into each other in prayer:

> *Even the sun goes down heroes eventually die*
> *Horoscopes often lie and sometimes "why"*
> *Nothin' is for sure nothin' is for certain nothin' lasts forever*
> *But until they close the curtain …*

WE DON'T REALLY SAY THAT WORD

On Thanksgiving,
Uncle drank too much
to tell my sisters and I apart
>*that word*,
>*pass me the salt*

I knew he meant me,
wore my new name like a gift
of second-day socks
maybe his,
maybe mine.

On the bus down Colorado Boulevard,
here came Cousin and Cousin,
drunk raucous funky loud laughing
>*that's why you my*
>**that word**

and me with my friends
hiding my face in my hands,
hoping they would not see me and
call me by my name.

On Auntie's birthday,
Uncle had too much
or not enough
>**that word**
>*give me back my ring*
>*before I take your finger off*

and Auntie was not having it
>*I ain't givin you shit*
>**that word**

and we all climbed out the back window.

We know when to wield words
and when to tiptoe.
We know whether laughter is an invitation
or a warning by its timbre,
same way we know that word.
Have washed its socks,
hung its drawers on the line,
made up the couch into a bed,
tucked it into the good sheets and
kept an eye out for morning.

BONES

1. You can keep your timid dreams.
   Short-breathed panting.
   Mediocre with fear.
   Tremble becomes a walk, a gait.
   Gate yourself safely
   but do not ask me to stay.

2. I am wild as spring.
   Fire that makes glass
   can melt it also.
   Bridges can be cages too.
   Let them all burn
   with old mirrors
   and doorknobs.

   You ever notice
   how they call it a rope
   burn? How binding rips
   into simple flesh and divorces
   the skin?

3. i have set fire to every photograph of every lover.
   maybe that is too far.
   lover.
   temporary as tampon, sterile in their regard,
   bleached as memory.

   this is how i cut the stain of you;
   rusted, unsightly fabric.
   stitched the hole left in my sheets,
   in my panties,
   until only a clean seam, or scar,
   reminds me that something happened there
   once.

when i was reminded to be humble.
when i was taught to be polite.
when i was raised to be a christian, all forgiveness and
    long-suffering.
when i was beaten into being a good girl. the best girl.
a girl that cuts her tongue from her mouth
and folds it into a quiet bouquet of blood.

4. I was married once. I said "I do"
   and meant it. Left my skeleton
   at the altar and shape-shifted
   into a beautiful apology.

   One year after the wedding, to the day,
   my gall bladder exploded inside my body.
   My gut was trying to form new bones
   from the waste.
   What a tragic way to love
   my fear more than myself.
   I have not done it since.
   Loved. Or should we call it
   suicide, the way I buried my own name
   in an unmarked grave
   in some winter
   where the ground will not yield
   for anything less than a hurricane's
   unearthing howl.

5. This is where I live, I say.
   This is my name, I say.
   These are the bones that belong to me.
   Some of them
   are yours.

IMITATION OF HOPE

"Why do they call him black when he's half white?"
she asks me at work and she is my boss and I like her
even if I am the only black person she knows
or half white, as she demands to assert casually
        (what is a half person?)
as if I would have gotten the job if I had come to the interview
with my unrepentant afro howling and whirling in the
        conference room
and not strangled into a comatose bun,
as if I can leave half of myself (from waist up or down?
        a split down the middle?)
waiting at the door reaching for bootstraps
        (what actually is a bootstrap?)
as if I didn't replace two people when they hired me,
as if they didn't replace me with three when I left,
as if we don't literally work twice as hard for half as much
(do they teach that gospel where you're from?).

"I PISSED!!!"
the hilariously mistyped subject line I receive
in response to my best friend's stepmother after
I "reply all" with unapologetic dissent to an email
she sent to everyone she knows to warn them about
Barack Hussein Obama

> *of course, he's a Muslim,*
> *of course, he's a Black Muslim,*
> *of course, he's not American,*
> *of course, he's not one of us,*
> *I mean you, I mean,*
> *I thought you were one of us,*
> *I mean, not us, but one of the good ones at least,*
> *I mean I thought I could trust you*
> *to take it, to eat it, to smile*
> *silent, I should have known*
> *one day all that black*
> *would slide out through that*
> *gap between your teeth,*
> *always hinting at something darker*
> *inside.*

I wept with my grandmother that election night.
I hoped it meant they didn't hate us
as much as they used to. I hoped it meant
I wasn't lying to my daughter anymore when I told her
she can be anything she wants when she grows up.

FDT

after election night

we went to the club

there was nothing left to do

but dance with our skin out

press against stronger bodies

drink in desperate smiles

questions of handsome strangers

stroke the soft beard of a man

you know a little and when

the DJ plays "Fuck Donald Trump"

the whole club explodes

we know we are on fire and burning

we dance until we are ashes

HOMEGIRL

Homegirl: Noun.

1. A girl or woman from one's own neighborhood or hometown.
In my neighborhood, women walk like they are their own
    favorite songs.
The way my beautiful aunties laugh and sway.
I am sure the world belongs to the music of their steps.
I practice this walk when no one is looking (*you ain't grown!*).
I watch the way my grandmother walks to her sister's house at night,
carrying a stick (for stray dogs, she tells us, or heavy-handed men
who refuse to leave) and praying all the way.
She tells us to stay together while we wait for her outside. We do.

2. An inner-city girl or woman.
I am 7 and the boy across the street calls me a homegirl.
We both think this is an insult.
My sister laughs, head-back and throaty, when I come home crying.

3. A girl or woman who is a friend.
In middle school, my best friend's father says
that everything north of a certain avenue
(where my house is) is a ghetto
and should be burned to the ground.
She and I argue about whether or not her father is racist.
I take everything the wrong way.

4. See: Around the Way Girl.
Lisa, Angela, Pamela, Renee.
LL Cool J praises the girls
with bamboo earrings and shining lip gloss.
My grandmother won't let me pierce my ears,
says marking up their bodies is the first sign
that people are separating themselves from God.
I am tucking hand-me-down bellbottoms into my socks
and praying no one sees.

5. A compound word made from "home" and "girl."
"DON'T NOBODY LIKE YOU ANYWAY, MYRON!"
my throat curling into a fist,
my legs pumping high noon,
I swing in a furious tornado at the boy
who pushed me off my bike, the roar and thrum
of my block boiling, beating him
into a wall of rosebushes. I bet
he still remembers my name, I hope
he feels a sting every time he balls a fist.

6. A female member of a peer group or gang.
My homegirl tells me about a man
breaking into her house
freshly after her divorce
when her children were little
and tucked into their beds.
She held the man at gunpoint
at her kitchen table,
brewed a pot of coffee
while they waited for police.

7. Plural noun: Homegirls.
My homegirls and I say homegirl like it belongs to us.
Like an invention or inheritance.
Either way, we've had that shit since like '85
    and we brought it with us.
A man broke my heart and my homegirl
    hexed his ass in a text message.
Ain't heard from him again.
A man broke my homegirl's heart and I swallowed his name.
Ain't heard from him again.
My homegirl made a fire in the backyard
    and we threw our dead into it.
We survived.
My homegirls and I "You Got to Get Through Me First."
My homegirls and I "How I Got Over."
Every other name too toothless to pass down to our daughters,
    who will carry
the sticks the crayons the fires the gloss the fists the roses the
    guns the coffee the men
the keys the babies the medicine the front doors the back doors
    the windows the words eachothereachothereachother.

ARS POETICA

I be fluent in my understanding of
you can't sit with us
but I'm eatin' anyway,
maybe in the kitchen
or maybe in the back yard
with the freshest chickens
find me in your coop
blood and quills and meat in my teeth
tell me whose shame this is
stuck to my cheeks
chickens can't fly
'cept in my mouth
become flesh of my flesh
watch what I make
with all these feathers
and shit.

SOME PEOPLE LIKE ME BETTER AS AN IDEA

the woman downtown in the coffee shop fills her face with alarm
you are the future I am afraid of
what if I am evaporating into the past

the woman on the elevator wants to know if I live here
what if I become everything
I have already suspected you are

the woman across the street calls the police to report my presence
why do you have to tell the whole Internet
every time these shaking fingers dial 911

the woman in the mail room wants to know how I got this job
can't this fear be between us
somebody's got to do something about all this fear

the woman at the suburban mall closes the door when she sees
      me approach
don't you feel me feeling it
isn't it your job to feel my feelings

the woman at the bar runs her hands through my hair
isn't that solidarity
don't you call that intersectional

the woman at the airport tries to cut the line
why can't you just stand a few blocks behind me
where I don't have to see you

the woman at the bar runs her hands along my backside
can't you be a little ugly or at least try
to be my version of pretty

the woman on the sidewalk afraid to look up
why don't you smile first or move out the way
why are you always in the way
why aren't you sorry for scaring me
what if I start to cry where will you hide
don't you know my tears get people like you killed

YOU CAN('T) TAKE US ANYWHERE

Me and B on the dance floor
with various other shades of people:

checkered flannel shirts cursive tattoos
lilting drunk belly out long legged
leather vest headband lace dress
what season even is this
heads bob eyes scan for heat

one spindly blonde hair swinging
in her face emerges from the throng
throws herself onto the wall spreads
arms out long wide pressing gyrating
her neck mostly but get it how you live

we are mostly swaying to hip hop hits
from the early 2000s they are mostly
the wrong ones we are hungry almost
begging for beats that demand our
sweat the dropping of hips

not these damn near slow jams
easy enough for the girl on the wall
unaffected by rhythm or any other
garden variety inebriate to interpret
into some kind of movement

meantime me and B so magic we invisible
arms crossed sullen salt in my stare
we don't check our coats to be insincere
I finally hear   *it's Bone and Biggie Biggie*
the opening bars   *it's Bone and Biggie Biggie*
to "Notorious Thugs"
yell "THAT'S MY SHIT"
me and B throw our hands in the air
                              ARMED AND DANGEROUS
                    AIN'T TOO MANY CAN BANG WITH US
and hold.

We are alive.
We are seen.
We point at the DJ
"I SEE YOU I SEE YOU" he sees us back
plays the JT Money classic "Who Dat"
and the asses commence to bounce now I know
I am loved give this glistening hype joy to the whole room
we shoulder roll body rock bouncing
live and electric even the air is ours until

I spin and see a tall drink of who-left-the-gate-open
wearing a trench coat he is standing alone in the corner
juggling glow-in-the-dark bowling pins
in the next corner a young lady hula-hooping
DJ is still playing JT Money and this might be the most
Denver shit I have ever seen in my life

B leans in to point at dude next to us
"he looks like ol' boy from *Don't Be a Menace*"
I am laughing so hard at the accuracy
I spin again so as not to hurt his feelings
then approaching from the door is a broad grin
white kid his hair dyed Kool-Aid red and
woven into dreadlocks the size of baguettes
they almost swing as he walks toward me
flashing his platinum grill I am howling B is
low twerking to keep from laughing too
I am hollering at the wind and the drum
that brought us here tonight.

When we make our exit
we are approached by a
clenched jaw big bodied
mostly shaved blond head
my fists tight for whatever
this is about to be he says
*"I'm sorry to bother but I just
really love your energy sorry I'm
tripping really hard right now
but I just had to tell you that"*
he folds his fist-chin into
his pocket-chest he means it.

On the ride home I laugh and lament
the precious disgust of the story my body told tonight:

arms crossed fist balling fight
hands up ass dropped surrender
impossible to sustain
impossible to defend
a home or a square inch of earth for a body or a breath
but sometimes, for the length of two songs, even the air is ours.

A PRIMARY EDUCATION IN SEX

1. we are in sixth grade, arguing
   about whether or not girls can cum.
   we both speak with authority
   neither of us has the distance
   to admit. she assures the slumber
   party that yes, they can.
   i insist that they cannot.
   we are both right.

2. my body is becoming even more a stranger.
   i am tangled in a bed of serpents.
   they are both murder and medicine,
   depending on the dose.
   my breasts swell to feed them.
   i leap from my skin and call it growth.

3. he wants me to look him in the eye.
   he wants me to say his name.
   he wants me to say it's his.
   i am still not sure it's mine.
   this precarious flesh curls in at the knuckle,
   which can look like an invitation.
   the remorse and retreat of my opening
   revolts and evicts even me.
   whose name to call on but God's?
   when a body won't behave
   like a lady, is a fistful of refusal?
   when some ambitious suitor stretches my vacant skin
   over his hands and calls it pretty?
   makes it dance?
   does not even notice it is empty?

ME TOO

"me too"
the woman in me rolls her eyes until she sees herself, untouched

"me too"
says every version of myself I've ever known

the child locked in a room
too small to reach the door's handle

the adolescent who did not know what boys do to girls who
        can't handle their liquor
the teenager who is afraid to hurt his feelings

the woman who says no and means it
but is not prepared to back it up

the woman who sleeps with a weapon under the pillow
because of what she has already learned about being unarmed in bed

the secretary who cries in the bathroom
the body grabbed at the bus stop at the party at the restaurant at
        the club

the account executive who outperforms her colleagues
(but only because she's pretty)

the 13- (going-on-30, they laugh, greasy-eyed) year-old girl
who clenches her fists

"me too"
almost every woman I know

"me too"
and so many of the men too

"me too"
so tired of all this still being true

"me too"
the woman in me rolls her eyes at all she has forgiven

CLUMSY-TONGUED LOVERS

he calls
        I'd be lying if I didn't admit
he says
        how much I have wanted my lovers
a woman
        to tongue their hearts slow
he tangled with
        let them soft melt
some time ago
        down my chin
is spinning some tales
            let their sweet tongues linger
him wanting more
        on my breast
than she offered
        like we can stay
but she offered
        wherever we are
he says
        indefinitely
until her boyfriend
            I admit
walked in
        their knowing of my body
and everything
        sober in the day
unraveled
        taught me something about love
but his waistband,
        our sharp and pulling commands
tightened
        come. here.

gripped

        take. that. off.

and yes

        don't. stop.

I know him

        a dance

love him even

        we know

when he is not mine

        say yes

this is not the first time

        say no

I have seen a man break

        say nothing at all

open into a new man

        for months

and yes

        even the current

I believe women

        of silence

and yes

        is a language

I know the spectrum   of assault

        also I know

enough to be a bad witness

        how to heal

damn right

        especially when

my body got calluses

        clumsy-tongued lovers

my body a stranger

        all messy mouthed

my lovers turn strangers

        do not know how to hear

HOW TO GET A MAN OUT OF YOUR HOUSE

Nana told us a story about a man
who once loved her,
who came to her house
with a machete and a suitcase
sharp enough, large enough
to cut and carry her pieces out in
but she looked at him squarely and said,
"I rebuke you, Satan, in the name of Jesus!"
and he turned, ran down the porch steps
like a skittish cat being shooed with a broom
and we all memorized and practiced reciting this phrase
in case we would need to use it one day.

LUCKY

"well, it looks like you're just gonna have to go ahead and do the two years"
looking past us over his glasses like we were already gone
with all the empathy of a pill bug rolling into itself
obvious and easy, tossing a used napkin
(and not a father) into a can
joylessly, mindlessly
like he does it every day
like my daughter invented her own face
and has no inheritance or ancestors to speak of.

> When I was a child, my breath would stop suddenly
> sometimes. It was like being choked. Went limp.
> Turned a pale blue. No one could explain it.

I spoke to the judge
in the crisp, starched, sheet-white
I have learned to serve when begging.

"he is lucky to have you, young lady"
Lucky, the way the color leaves my face.
Lucky, how this pliant flesh becomes armor, like it was trained.
Lucky, how flat my tone becomes when pressed.
Lucky, how fluently I play dead.

THE HOUSE OF JOY

Nana got my good shoes in her purse
'cause we walk waaaaaaay down Martin Luther King Boulevard
    to church.
I yawn, rub my eyes. Last night, she saved my head for last
because my hair gives her the most trouble and will not lay down
in spite of heat and Blue Magic by the handful.
"It's going to take prayer and relaxer."

When we lived with our mom, we never went to church,
Nana laments, reminds us to pray for her. "Thank God I have
    you now."

We are obedient patent leather shoes, polishing out the scuff.
We are children's choir.
We are names in the family Bible.

At church, everyone is beautiful and strange.
Pastor Beechum's chest is booming as his voice builds into
frenzy, desperate to save us all from the fiery pit awaiting
sinners.

Nana is standing up, shaking her Bible and pointing to it,
"Uh-Uh! That's not THE WORD"
Pastor hollering "THIS IS MY CHURCH!"
Nana shouting "WELL I ONLY GO TO GOD'S CHURCH!"
We are ushered back out onto Martin Luther King Boulevard
    before the service is over.

Sister Gussy gives us sandwiches for the walk home.
2 slices of bread, 1 slice of cheese, no meat or mustard or
    Miracle Whip,
but we say "thank you" anyway because Nana always tells people
we are well behaved and know our manners.

"I've been kicked out of better places than this,"
Nana's covered head, her indignant tooth suck, a Sunday
    morning beacon.
We are leaping over cracked sidewalks in hopeful prayer.

We are paper fans, printed with funeral home advertisements,
    dancing in unison.
We know better than to laugh when someone gets the Holy Ghost.
We are Jesus' favorite.

THE GOD CONJURERS SING

The God Conjurers Sing
and their faces contort
into Magnificent exorcism and we
are all saved, saved again
                              clap   clap-clap
                              clap   clap-clap

Lifted by some holy Holy
Spirit, always shows up for the singing
and who wouldn't? This Sweat
ghost dancing a most perfect prayer,
Hallelujah Anyhowing
and Praise-His-Holy-Name-ing too,
                              clap   clap-clap
                              clap   clap-clap

We contort and invoke breastbone-shaking song
for ourselves as much as we ever did for God;
expect God got plenty music
all over Heaven
and here We come, harmonizing
                              clap   clap-clap
                              clap   clap-clap

The Church has no air conditioning;
shoo the devil's heat out windows,
nobody wants to admit how hot it is in here
when Pastor keeps talking about hell, so we Sing
a Fever and keep hold to our cool,
                              clap   clap-clap
                              clap   clap-clap

Sweating halos and Surviving
everything we brought here with us,
hoping to lay it down, bury
our Sorrow with some kind of Grace
                            clap   clap-clap
                            clap   clap-clap

we know these Rhythms,
know how to holler out from the Dark
                            clap   clap-clap
and be saved
again, Witness and Praise
the Miracle of voice
                            clap   clap-clap
We yellow Lanterns
fighting to glow in a Storm,
                            clap   clap-clap

Hallelujah Anyhow
                            clap   clap-clap

Praise-His-Holy-Name
                            clap   clap-clap

We Are Still Here
and Holy

THE BLUE NOTE BENDS 'TIL BREAKING

We play the black keys.
Press fingers into guitar strings and quiver into callus.
We play the hollows, the echo of our slapping tells the story of wind.

Maybe hurricanes are how our ancestors return home.
Maybe they take us with them in pieces,
breathing and drinking all this dust and bone.

We moan a map to be remembered.
We howl as well as we hymn. A chorus. An opera. A medley.
We are born knowing how to sing.

We coax shadows out of hiding with a long, low note.
We stare until our trembling is more vibrato than fear.
Our voices grow even in silence.

ÉOSTRE

mothers know magic;
understand eggs;
the left and right breast
and how to use each;
how to fold someone into a body
and pull them out, new.

mothers sing gospel
while they wash dishes;
praise for the hot water,
running easy.
hallelujah, the plates were messed
and everybody ate.

mothers laugh silently
and curse
without saying a word.

see? there is something there now.
you did not see it before.

MUSTANGS

"I been really tryyyyyyin baby
tryna hold back this feelin for sooooo long
and if you feel
like i feel, baby
come on
oh, come on"

Janis Hunter was a 17-year-old high school student
when 34-year-old Marvin Gaye crooned her open.
When you type "Janis Hunter" into Wikipedia,
it forcibly redirects to Marvin Gaye's page.
He is, after all, the only reason we know her name.
When you Google Janis Hunter, the first result is the headline:
"Marvin Gaye's Wife Reveals How He Tortured Her."
She still speaks of loving him. Does she still have a name?

Lori Mattix was a 15-year-old virgin
when 27-year-old David Bowie groomed her wide open
for Jimmy Page to follow, then Mick Jagger,
who sang to her of wild horses.

And of course, young girls are mustangs –
    from the Spanish "mustengo,"
      meaning ownerless beast –
mustangs have no natural predators
but the men who catch and break them.

    "Childhood living is easy to do"

To break a wild horse, first you must gain its trust.
Sing to it. Call it pretty until you mount.
Get the reins on quickly; wild beasts must be controlled from
        the head.
Give it a new name. Something easy for you to say, like "Baby."
She will forget she ever owned the wind.

I was 13 when the first man-boy tried to tell me he loved me.
He was 20. I pretended not to hear him and hung up.

I was 15 when the second man-boy tried to tell me he loved me.
He was 20. I pretended not to hear him and hung up.

I was 16 when the third man-boy tried to tell me he loved me.
He was much older than 20. I pretended not to hear him and
        hung up.

And how they loved me.
Called me muse, watching me playful in open fields.
    "Fame, makes a man take things over. ..."

Called me quiet, teasing with handfuls of oats.
    "Fame, what you want is in the limo. ..."

Called me beautiful until I stopped kicking.
Called me theirs. Called it love.
    "Is it any wonder?"

Say:
"There's nothing wrong with me lovin you"
"There's nothing wrong with me lovin you"
"There's nothing wrong with me lovin you"
Say it like a mantra until it feels true
      until the saddle feels like skin
      until the yoke feels like religion
  "There's nothing wrong with me
  lovin' you. ..."

Does love mean to lasso a feral mare?
Does love ride bareback and call itself quick?
Does love mean to harness the thunder in my hips until it all
  feels yours?
Does love always catch around the throat
or as a bit in the mouth
like so?

The first time I told a man I loved him,
I coughed up a rusted chain and a collar.
I traced it with my tongue and found my own name
already engraved there, just below my mother's.

  "Wild, wild horses, we'll ride them some day. ..."

SWEETBACK

When Chris Dorner trained his gun
on the LAPD, when he released
a manifesto addressed
        To: America
        Subject: Last Resort
we knew it was clearly a suicide note.
I take no joy in the blood on his hands
nor his burnt body
but it comes as no great shock
that some policemen
look like overseers
even now.

So, yes.
When he quoted D. H. Lawrence,
"I never saw a wild thing feel sorry for itself,"
I wanted to tell him to run.
Not because he was innocent,
but even the foreshadow of defeat
is enough to awaken the adrenaline
when your bones remember the burning.
I wanted to tell him to run.
Not for himself, nor his own iron hands
but for Fred Hampton
and Malcolm X
and Martin Luther King, Jr.
and Amadou Diallo
and Troy Davis
and Trayvon Martin
and Paul Childs
and Ramarley Graham
and Sean Bell
and Oscar Grant

and Rekia Boyd
and Timothy Stansbury
and Orlando Barlow
and Aaron Campbell
and Victor Steen
and Steven Washington
and Alonzo Ashley
and Wendell Allen
and Aiyana Jones
and Ronald Madison
and Marvin Booker
and James Brissette
and John Crawford III
and Eric Garner
and Barbara Dawson
and Mike Brown
and Tamir Rice
and Walter Scott
and Cameron Tillman
and Eric Harris
and Sandra Bland
and Alton Sterling
and Philando Castile
and Alva Braziel
and so many more names
that I will never know

and I did not know
any of these people
but damned if they couldn't all been my family
and I know they say it's not a war
but damned if I don't feel like an insurgent sometimes
and no, I have never killed anyone,
but have long since admitted
that I could.

I mean, America, you got big guns.
I ain't scared, though, not with this working womb.
America, you thought the Black Panther
Free Breakfast Program was scary,
you ain't met me yet.

We've been through a lot, America.
I think that now, for every one of our children
you allow to be murdered, I will make two.
With brothas gully as they come.
All grit and swagger and knuckle and earth and gleam,
beards all unapologizing.
Brothas who won't smile at you.
Brothas who ain't never been afraid of you.
Brothas who smell just like the sun.

We will raise our babies together, like militia, ticking.
We will detonate them on your college campuses,
at your job, in your neighborhood.
We will suck up all the financial aid.
We will teach Fred Hampton in the classrooms
until his blood can stop screaming.

You don't want it with we, America.
We, Black mothers, are angry as ever,
are fertile as ever, and unafraid
of our children.

I'm not leaving, America.
We will take over the schools and
send your daughters home smiling
like Patty Hearst, America.
You feeling me now?
You fearing me now?

I might even have your babies, America.
They will be Black, too.

America, this is a war.
America, I will send my sons to all your corners.
You will be needing their light.

America, this is no manifesto. This is a love poem.
Making love is the only way I know how to save you.
Your hatred and fear are a cancer.
Your teeth are rotting from your head.

America, now is the time
to call on whatever God you pray to.
Give thanks for my brilliant sons.
Yes, there will be sons, Black sons.
We will call them all Jamal and Rakim
and we will love them. We will love them.

We're not dying, America.
We will live forever.

LOAD

I do not have a gun.
I would not admit this out loud,
except that you will not know
when you read this
whether or not it's still true.

I used to joke
"I don't have a gun
for the same reason I don't have credit cards:
I would use them,"
but I have credit cards now. I use them.

You know how bullets whistle before they die?
You know how they die in a thud?
You know how a man screams when he is split?
You know how blood sprints?

I laugh at guns in movies, how quick and clean,
weightless at the end of a weak wrist.
Real guns pinch and kick before they bite.
Real guns do not like being laughed at –
would bloody my mouth, knock it clean off.

You know how you lean a rifle against your shoulder
and keep a little flex in your elbow, right?
You know how a shotgun sprays?
How to bend your knees and lean in while you take aim?

You know you only take your shot
when you are certain of what you will hit, don't you?
Didn't anybody ever tell you that?
How we don't waste bullets or fire at things we don't plan to kill?

You know a thing can be living
and then not?
How it can happen in a click?

Real guns know about time and movement.
Real guns know about speed and weight.
Real guns know about straight lines and splatter.

You know how guns have bad manners sometimes?
How they ignore guest lists and invitations?
How they interrupt?

ON THE DAY YOU VISIT A SLAUGHTERHOUSE

The men that you work with, all older, all whiter,
all watching for the color to drain from your face,
wanting to tell the story back at the office about how you cry-vomited
(you could not possibly be cut out for the same work that they are,
not with those fleshy breasts and supple thighs, not with those
kinks in your woolly hair, not with that vegetarian mouth)
will nudge each other in the ribs, quietly pointing,
stunned that you accepted the dare.

Of course you did. You had to. Square your shoulders,
remember you are made of the same bone and blood.
Smile at their boyish wonder. Pretend they are your children,
it makes them easier to forgive. They will think they are the first
to stare, to point and snicker. Of course, you have been playing
this game all your life. Of course you will know how to win it.

You will smell the fear from miles away, the wind full of blood and
    waste.
You will want to turn around. You will not be able to move.
You will stand neck to neck with the cowboys
as they joke about their "harvest," their eyes, daring you to judge them.
You will accept.

You will find that the first room is almost easy,
a steel bowl the size of your apartment
catching all the ground pieces of cattle that no one wanted to buy.
You will almost love the bowl for holding them,
like a mother, before they make their way to a mouth.
This is a tender moment between you and the bowl.

The second room is easier still: steaks, packed in stacks of boxes.
Pretend that they are gift wrapped, that they are saving a life,
remind yourself that we all make sacrifices, even of ourselves.
Remember the times that you have given blood, decide that this is the
    same thing.
Tell yourself you are one with the cows.
Of course you are.

The third room is where the meat is graded.
This is the first indication that it was once something walking,
full sides of beef hanging from hooks in the ceiling, it almost looks like
    dancing.
They will ask you to admire the fat content, they will call it "marbling."
You will lean in, hoping to hear how painless a death, how pleasant a life,
but you will know too much about feedlots.

When you finally step onto the "kill floor," you will pretend that you
    are in a movie.
It is the only way to walk through a river of blood without trying to
    save someone.
You will see lungs, and hearts, lone eyeballs rolling along the conveyor
    belt
like tumbleweed; you will not ask where they are going.
You will see the system of undoing:

Slice off the hoof.
Slice off the hoof.
Slice off the hoof.
The cattle, dangling from the hooks, moving down the line.
Peel back the skin.
Peel back the skin.
Peel back the skin.
Their bodies will still be warm and bleeding.
Pluck out the eye.
Pluck out the eye.
Pluck out the eye.

When you enter the final room, you will see each cow fresh from its kill.
Tongues hanging from their slack mouths.
Their eyes will be open.
They will all be looking at you.

You will have to decide what part of yourself you are going to kill now.
It is the only way to keep yourself from giving them names.
Decide their lives are only worth the price you'll sell them for.
This is why you are here.
This is how you feed your daughter.

When you walk up to the roof of the slaughterhouse,
you will see them marching rows of cattle to their death.
You will see each cow smell the blood and back away.
You will see the cowboys frighten them forward.
You will know that you are a cowboy.
You will want to cry.

When they take you to the boardroom for lunch, they will serve prime rib.
It will bleed all over everyone's plate but yours.
You will know that your coworkers are right, you do not belong here.
This is why they look at you like you are already quivering on their plates,
why they begin reciting recipes every time you enter a room.

DIVORCE CAKE: A RECIPE

Serves One.

Ingredients:
1 cup butter, softened
Your 3 favorite albums
3 cups white sugar
Stacks of photographs
7 eggs
1 hammer
1 tablespoon vanilla extract
1 cigarette lighter
3 cups all-purpose flour
1 pair scissors
¼ teaspoon baking powder
1 ball of twine
¼ teaspoon baking soda
1 pen
1 cup sour cream
1 notebook

Directions:
1. Preheat oven to 325 degrees F (165 degrees C). Grease and flour a 9x13-inch pan or a 10-inch Bundt pan.
2. Select the album you most want to sing along to, and play it loud.
3. In a large bowl, cream together the butter and sugar.
4. Spread the photographs on the living room floor. Study each face to determine who expected failure and blame them. Seek the fools who believed and stare at them, bewildered at the distance between each photo's congratulating gloss and the hollow way your voice sounds now.

5. Choose the photograph that best represents your shame. With the lighter firmly in hand, set it aflame, and drop it into the sink. Watch it burn.
6. Choose the photograph that best represents your foolish hope. Use the scissors to cut out your face, and create a small hole at the top. Thread the twine through the hole, and hang it above the door.
7. Return to the kitchen. Beat the eggs into the butter and sugar mixture one at a time, mixing well after each.
8. Take the hammer to your bedroom. Collapse into your neatly tucked sheets. Spread your limbs across the full width of your bed. Wrap your fingers tightly around the hammer. Lift it; note the imbalance of its weight. Tuck the hammer under your pillow. You will feel safer when sleeping alone.
9. Remind yourself that you are still making a cake. Stir the vanilla into the egg, butter, and sugar mixture and let the fragrance remind you of being a child.
10. Combine the flour, baking soda, and baking powder, add to the creamed mixture and mix until all of the flour is absorbed.
11. Select the album that conjures the face of your young, foolish love. Play it louder than the first.
12. Finally, stir in the sour cream until the lumps disappear.
13. Weep into the batter until your shoulders shake and heave. Pour the batter into the prepared pan.
14. Select the album that you once loved together. Play it softly. Sing along.
15. Bake the smooth and salty batter in the preheated oven for 45 to 60 minutes, or until a toothpick inserted into the center of cake comes out clean.
16. Decide whether to remove the cake from the oven, or let it burn awhile. You will know when it's ready.
17. Drown the cake pan in soapy water. Leave it in the sink for three days. Throw it away if you want to. It was probably a wedding gift anyway.

18. Take the pen. Sign the papers. Write a letter to yourself so you remember this moment.
19. Call your best friends. Ask them to bring you a tub of frosting. Eat the frosting by the spoonful, or fling it against the walls. List the fears about what happens now, all stirring in your cakeless belly.
20. Buy a cake. Eat it all.

CECIL

and are we not lions?
are we not the roar of an unanswered fire?
are we not holding the sun in our manes?

are we not born quick-toothed jawing?
are we not stalking survival with every midnight and morning?
are we not endangered?

are we not pride?
are we not crowns?
are we not your primal fear, encapsulated?

are we not hunted?
are we not mounted trophies in bedrooms?
are we not worn as costume?

are we not game?
are we not impressive photographs?
are we not the best stories you've ever told?

are we not mighty?
are we not untenable hunger?
are we not the racing of your pulse?

are we not boundless?
are we not stealth?
are we not daily guarding our children?

are we not what you call savage?
are we not the burning threat of sun?
are we not bled for gold?

are we not hated for the birthright of our dignity?
are we not broad chests?
are we not heads held high?

are we not lions?
are we not the bruise of curiosity?
are we not ripped open?

I FALL IN LOVE AT MUSEUMS

I walk into paintings.

Sometimes I don't come back.
Art is like that, you know.

Lovers get jealous
of the places they can't follow me to,
afraid of facing the loss
or becoming it.

Who wouldn't, really?

Haven't you been stranded in a gray ocean
or on the stem of a purple flower before?

Don't you lose your way when your heart is captured?

MY STEPFATHER IS NOT THE KIND OF MAN WHO WEEPS

When we heard that your mother was dying,
we stood in silence until the truth rooted itself into our back teeth
and all we could taste was the silent agony of knowing.
I heaved the big skillet onto the flame,
coaxed the Crisco down from the top of the pantry,
dropped generous spoonfuls until it shined a welcome.

This is how we family sometimes.
Grandmothers whispering in paprika pinches and dry mustard dash,
recipe woven into creases of calloused hands.
A cluster of collards cooked slow when we need to still.
A touch of cumin or cayenne when it is time again to move.
A peeled potato for every word caught just behind a throat's tickle.

My stepfather is not the kind of man who weeps.
He stares into the mossy grass, silently says:
Earth, if you open your mouth and call me home
I will fold easy into your sturdy batter,
I will swell and stiffen to a cake of you, and I will rest.
His shoulders do not shake.

I DO NOT KNOW HOW TO LOVE YOU IN ENGLISH

I cannot tell by its rhythm where this heart was born,
it is only music pulsing through palms.
We know this when we hold hands,
let whispers tickle ears
whatever language they assume.

I do not know how to cry in English
    No sé cómo llorar en Español
tears are born world citizens
they do not need to speak to find each other,
to rush into rivers that cannot be dammed.

I will not ask the wind where it is from;
it would only answer
with its coming and going,
does not recognize these fences or lines,
does not even see them.

I will not ask the Monarchs for a passport,
will not pinch them from the air
and pin them for their passage,
will not shoot them
as they fly away.

I will not shush the roaring seas
beating upon the border from another nation's shore
will not pretend its origin is worth less or more,
we are each of us worth our weight in water
or *en papeles*.

I will not ask each grain of sand
from whence it came,
will not interrogate the sediments
and segregate them by shade,
I will not cast a net around the beaches.

I do not know how to love you in English
    No sé cómo te amo en Español;
only know that all life begins with love
that cannot be walled or conquered.
I will not ask love where it is from;
Only know that it resides in me,
in the *descansos* dotting the desert.

I do not know what language bullets speak
have only ever heard them whisper past my head
in words I do not wish to remember or repeat;

Would rather press palm to palm and whisper poems
    "Give us your tired, your poor, your huddled masses
    yearning to breathe free. ..."

Would rather smile, warm as stew-filled belly
and break bread.

I will not ask the flames I cook with
for identification
when they burn more orange
than red, white,
or blue

as I do not know how to eat in English
> *No sé cómo comer en Español;*

I do not know how to breathe in English
> *No sé cómo respirar en Español;*

I do not know how to bleed in English
> *No sé cómo sangrar en Español;*

but I think it is the same
> *Creo que es lo mismo*

Con mis palabras
y con mi lengua rota
yo trato hablar.

> *With my words*
> *and with my broken tongue*
> *I try to speak.*

FOR CEDRIC

During senior year of high school,
a boy that I grew up with was shot at a local shopping mall.
A girl at school I had never spoken to approached me,
concern in her brow, asking sweetly, "How's your friend?"
I was moved by her empathy, an exotic bird
in a beige land of suburban track houses.
I answered, "He's still in critical condition, but we're all praying.
My grandmother is down at the hospital now."
She, head bobbing hair flip, smile shifting into quiet knife replied,
"Well, I still say if he was a gang member, he deserved to get shot."

This poem is for Michelle Albright, and what we deserve.

You deserved both of my hands around your throat that day,
and the shaking I gave you.
You probably still live in some suburb somewhere,
in a house just like the one you grew up in.
You are probably married to some insurance agent who played
high school ball and still reminisces when he drinks too much
on the weekends.
You are probably a banker. One of those predatory mortgage
lenders who gets rich by manipulating poor people.
You probably have two kids who look exactly like you.
You probably think that they deserve the best.

Michelle, you never knew Cedric.
You never saw the bruises he or his sister wore to Sunday school.
You never tried not to fall asleep at the all-night prayer sessions
the adults in our families held in hopes of protecting them
from their stepfather, never prayed for him to get "saved,"
never curled inside the kindness of their mother,
never grew roots in the forest of her song.
You did not come to our reunions or revivals,
never heard the desperation in our melody.
You have never been unable to afford
the arrogance of your godlessness.

Michelle, you never saw Cedric smile.
You never tried to beat him in a foot race.
You never wept or prayed for him.
You never knew why his manhood was so urgent,
or why it cost him so much blood to achieve.

Michelle, I want you to know that he did survive.
And that when he recovered, he reclaimed himself the only way
      he knew how.
That he was seventeen when they locked him away for good.
And that the last time I saw him was his mother's funeral.
We were eighteen then.
They did not unshackle his hands nor his feet as he rattled to
the pulpit to read a poem he had written for his dead mother,
and all I could think about
was you, and what you said he deserved.

Michelle, I still see his aunties and uncles and cousins sometimes.
He is his family's phantom limb, but I know better than to stare
or talk about it, my family has missing teeth of its own.

Michelle, I am a mother now.
Every night, when I listen at my daughter's door
I can tell – through the door – the difference between asleep
breathing, awake breathing, and awake-pretending-to-be-asleep
    breathing.
I have kissed her head and toes, cleaned her messes, read her books,
wrote her lullabies, taught her to ride a bicycle and to swim,
cheered at graduations and field days and spelling bees,
helped with homework, talked down teachers,
spoken to the mothers of bullies, spoken to bullies,
prayed and prayed and prayed.

Michelle, I taught her to read, taught her to speak, to speak up
even to me, I have washed and matched her socks over and over
    again,
have had to send her out into a world that does not value her life,
that would tell her something about inferiority and it belonging
    to her,
about her body and identity and it belonging to them,
that pretends that black lives are not as carefully cultivated as
    white lives,
as if she is not the most loved child that has ever lived.

Michelle, I wonder what you think she deserves?
Michelle, I know Cedric's mother felt the same way about her son
that I do about my daughter,
Michelle, what do you teach your babies?
Michelle, do you know what a victim is? Do they always look
    like you?
Michelle, have you ever felt like a statistic?
Michelle, did you know they make whole juries just like you?
Michelle, did you know the smack of a gavel can crack a spirit in half?
Michelle, do you have a spirit?
Michelle, we all deserve better than this.
Even you.

MY FATHER'S HANDS

the sun was 3:30 low
and hot
and so and so
had said such and such
about our mama
or our daddy
and we couldn't say
for sure
whether or not
it was true,
but we rolled four deep
and were not
going easy,
so when the mob
of children met us
at the corner
we were ready,
all of us,
with our father's hands
balled into stone and swing,
our grandmother's holler
talking slick and mean
from each mouth,
our mother's laugh
canyons away
from us.

We were born to fight.
We did not learn.
We have always known.
Even when everyone was bigger and more,
the hands knew how to fist,
the holler knew when to howl,
the laughter knew when to grimace
into menacing forgiveness, disguised in a smile.
This is true.
This is science.
This is the holiest magic.

One long night
so late it would have been morning,
the sun swallowed its own face.
In fact, all of the light
had gone from the world.
These father hands were dead fish,
this grandmother holler a choke,
this mother laugh a hunting hyena.

Some hands
bigger than my hands
some holler bigger
than my holler,
some laugh bigger than my
begging,
some want
bigger
than my God
of knuckles
and bite.

I put my hands in my mouth
and chewed,
reached down into my throat
and pulled.
I sat like this,
useless hands and holler,
endlessly swallowing my sounds.

I became
an eternity of whispers,
a heaven of new fingers,
the echo of my own open mouth.

BLACK RAGE IN FOUR-PART HARMONY

I.

I am easy black,
indie black,
light black,
like black light,
your black friend,
(so cliché),
your only black employee;

want me to be your soundtrack,
want me to give you permission,
want to touch my hair,
want to end-of-summer compare skin tones
(I always lose),
still blacker than you;

you will follow me through the store,
offer to hold my things at the counter
until I am ready to check out,
but you will still ride the elevator
and will probably not clutch your purse.

I listen to gangster rap
loud
with the windows down
when I drive through your neighborhood.
I have stolen your boyfriends
on purpose
or at least glances from them
to shame you.
I have balled up my tongue
into Gatling gun
spit sour nickels into a sack
and hit you with it
it never lashes
the same way as
nigger
no matter how hard I whip my words.

II.

My grandmother instructed us
all hard molasses
the first time strangers referred to us as
"negro" children.
It was a word we had not heard before.
"Around this house, we are black."
She spoke easy as
hot comb, smoking,
smooth Blue Magic
sharp surprise of burnt ears
and stinging "sit still!"

Around our Sunday afternoon table
we used to smile into each other's black faces,
we laughed magnificent black and
loved each other with an unbreakable blackness.

We blacked music and ate to its rhythm,
blacked mismatched dishes,
blacked each other's hair and fingernails,
blacked double-dutch and song,
blacked yes, please,
blacked no, thank you,
blacked only the most delicious black,
all the time, blacking.

My mother still wants to believe
that I could white the same way,
a flash of teeth,
a sprinkle of freckle.

I tell her that most white people
only want me white
when they want to win an argument.

Strangers still ask me sometimes
what I am.
They often preface the question with
"I mean, I can see you have some
black in you."
I laugh, blackly,
not minding the question so much
as their expectation of an answer.

I am the end of the pool
that no one is afraid of
until the bottom drops out.
Sometimes this light skin gets me invited to parties
that I am not really welcome at.

III.

Why you so mad?
Why you so mad?
Why you got a chip on your shoulder?
Why you so mad?
Why you can't just
swallow stones
'til you stop being hungry?
Why you can't just smile?
Why you can't just dance?
Why you can't just drink?
I mean, we made you an exception,
we let you slide,
we might even let you pass
so why you gotta be so mad?
Why you got your chest
puffed up
after we put the fire hoses away?
Why you can't just
shake your head and
suck your teeth and
look to your own and forget
that everybody is your own?
Why you can't just keep it pushin'?
Why you can't just shuck?
Why you can't just shrug?
Why you can't just laugh?
We were only joking
all "present company excluded"
all "but you're not like that"
I mean, all I said was ghetto,
all I said was ratchet,
all I said was nappy,
why you can't just relax?

Why you can't just press and curl?
Why you can't just pop your bootie?
Why you can't just drop it?
Everybody's droppin' it.
Why you so mad?
Why you so mad?
Why you so mad?
Why you so black?

IV.

There are three basic ways to make a noose.
The first is to run the tail of the rope through a fixed loop.

The second, and most common way,
is to tie a simple knot round the standing part of the rope.
When pulled, the knot side closes the loop,
the heel of a hand pressed against an easy throat,
a gate left foolishly swinging open.

The third is the same as the second, except that pulling the knot
will open the loop like the string on a yo-yo.
This is usually only done by mistake.

This is not a promise,
only finger and thumb
unraveling.

A tongue, tying and untying.
Interlaced fingers
and knots.

It is hushed whispers
over a fledgling tree
that everyone knows
was watered with blood
'cept, of course, the tree.
Wonders why her arms grow out
so snatching,
why she shake them loose when they
fool enough to climb,
menacing into her afro leaves,
why everyone knows
she is too hungry a place
for their children
to swing.

Black people,
once free,
did not
gather in mobs
and hunt,
despite all the same access
to trees
and rope.

ABOUT THE AUTHOR

Suzi Q. Smith is an award-winning artist, activist, and educator who lives in Denver, Colorado.

Her poems have appeared in *Union Station Magazine*, *Suspect Press*, *La Palabra*, *Muzzle Magazine*, *Malpaís Review*, *The Pedestal*, *The Los Angeles Journal*, *Denver Syntax*, *Word Is Bond*, *The Peralta Press*, *Yellow Chair Review*, and in the anthologies *The Mutiny Info Reader*, *DiverseCity*, *His Rib: Anthology of Women*, and *In Our Own Words*. Her chapbook collection of poems, *Thirteen Descansos*, was published by Penmanship Books in 2015. Currently, Suzi Q. is at work on her next collection while she continues to teach Creative Writing and cultivate a beautiful life.

AUTHOR THANKS

(this should be read while swaying to
the rhythm of a double clap):

To my beloved friends Ken Arkind, Tongo Eisen-Martin, Bobby LeFebre, Bianca Mikahn, Confidence Omenai, Lady Speech Sankofa, who have held these poems from their earliest moments. To my careful and candid writing group, including Thuyanh Asbury, Tameca L. Coleman, D. L. Cordero, Steven Dunn, Alexandrea Jackson, Ajha Fox, Brian Lupo, Joe Ponce, and to all of the dear friends who have spent time with these poems, helping me to see and love them more clearly. To my teachers who became mentors and friends, Barry Cummings and Wayne Gilbert, for helping me believe in my own voice. To Terrance Hayes for the Advanced Workshop at Lit Fest 2018, where I began to take these poems more seriously, and to Lighthouse Writers Workshop. To the poets who language against erasures. To the writers who have made a way for me. To the people who love me through it all, especially those who know how I disappear into books and love me still when I emerge. Thank you, thank you, thank you.

ACKNOWLEDGMENTS

- "We Pay Cash for Houses" first appeared in *Suspect Press*, Winter 2018.
- "Bones" first appeared in *Suspect Press*, September 2016.
- "Sweetback" first appeared in *No Dear Magazine*, February 2016.
- "My Father's Hands" first appeared in Muzzle Magazine, November 2013.
- "I Do Not Know How to Love You in English" first appeared in *Malpaís Review*, June 2012.
- "Bones" and "Mustangs" first appeared in *Mutiny Info Reader*, November 2016.
- "My Stepfather Is Not the Kind of Man Who Weeps" first appeared in *Diverse-City Anthology*, April 2013.

SONG LYRICS

- "Return of the 'G'" by OutKast
- "SpottieOttieDopaliscious" by OutKast
- "Hold On, Be Strong" by OutKast
- "Liberation" by OutKast
- "Slump" by OutKast
- "Mamacita" by OutKast
- "Y'all Scared" by OutKast
- "Aquemini" by OutKast
- "West Savannah" by OutKast
- "Da Art of Storytellin'" by OutKast
- "Notorious Thugs" by The Notorious B.I.G.
- "Let's Get It On" by Marvin Gaye
- "Wild Horses" by The Rolling Stones
- "Fame" by David Bowie

COLOPHON

The edition you are holding is the First Edition of this publication.

The title is set in Antraste, created by Marco Ballarè. The sans serif font is set in Avenir Book, created by Adrian Frutiger. The Alternating Current Press logo is set in Portmanteau, created by JLH Fonts. All other text is set in Iowan Old Style, created by John Downer. All fonts used with permission; all rights reserved.

Cover artwork designed by Leah Angstman, with elements by Brigitte at Art Tower. The Alternating Current lightbulb logo created by Leah Angstman, ©2013, 2021 Alternating Current. All images used with permission; all rights reserved.

Other Works from
ALTERNATING CURRENT PRESS

All of these books (and more) are available at
Alternating Current's website: press.alternatingcurrentarts.com.

alternatingcurrentarts.com